SOMETIMES

Bad Things

HAPPEN

Ellen Jackson
Photographs by Shelley Rotner

THE MILLBROOK PRESS
BROOKFIELD, CONNECTICUT

Sometimes
bad things
happen. You
may feel sad,
scared, hurt,
or angry.

Your game is
canceled
because of rain.

Your brother tells
you that a
bully pushed him.

Grown-ups fight.

You see scary
news stories on
television.

A few people do
bad things.

But most people
want to make
the world a
better place for
everyone.

These people
build homes for
the homeless.

They rescue
people who
have been hurt.

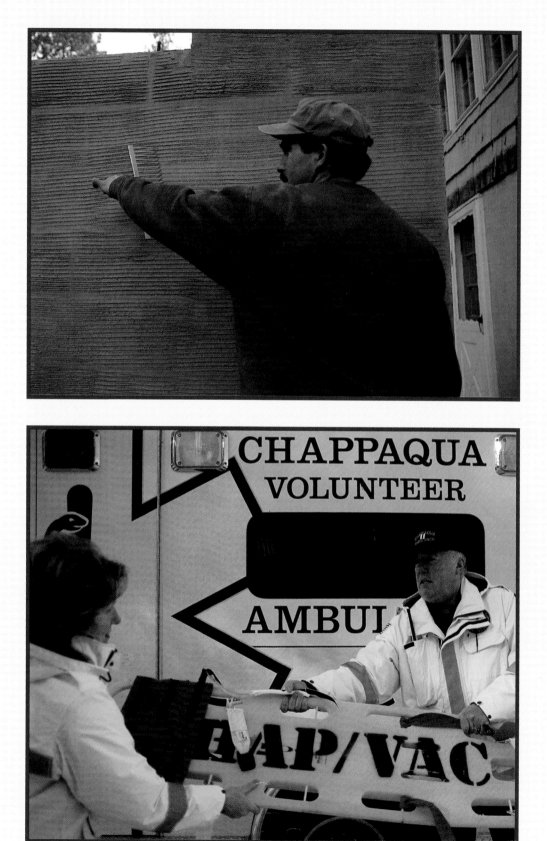

They care for
animals.

Or help children
feel safe.

When you are
sad, scared, hurt,
or angry, think
about the good
people you know.

When bad things
happen . . .

Hug a friend.

Plant a flower.

Listen to a poem.

Kick a ball.

Look up at the sky.

Sing a brave song.

Help someone.

It's okay to cry.
And very soon . .

Something good
will happen.

It always does.

To Dick Cousineau and Judy Freeman —EJ
To everyone whose lives will never be the same after September 11th. —

Copyright © 2002 by Ellen Jackson
Photographs copyright © 2002 by Shelley Rotner

Published by
The Millbrook Press, Inc.
2 Old New Milford Road
Brookfield, Connecticut 06804
www.millbrookpress.com

Printed in the United States of America

Library 1 3 5 4 2
Pbk 1 3 5 4 2

Library of Congress Cataloging-in-Publication Data
Jackson, Ellen B., 1943–
Sometimes bad things happen/Ellen Jackson ; photographs by Shelley
Rotner.
p. cm.
Summary: Mentions some of the bad things that happen in the world and
presents some positive ways to respond to them.
ISBN 0-7613-2810-6 (lib. bdg.)
1. Stress in children—Juvenile literature. 2. Stress management for
children—Juvenile literature. [1. Consolation.] I. Rotner, Shelley,
ill. II. Title.
BF723.S75 J33 2002
155.9—dc21   2001007510